IMAGES OF WAR

THE ARMOUR OF ROMMEL'S AFRIKA KORPS

RARE PHOTOGRAPHS FROM WARTIME ARCHIVES

Ian Baxter

Pen & Sword
MILITARY

First published in Great Britain in 2018 by
PEN & SWORD MILITARY
An imprint of
Pen & Sword Books Ltd
47 Church Street
Barnsley
South Yorkshire
S70 2AS

ISBN 978-1-52672-239-3

Typeset by Concept, Huddersfield, West Yorkshire HD4 5JL.
Printed and bound in England by CPI Group (UK) Ltd, Croydon CR0 4YY.

Pen & Sword Books Limited incorporates the imprints of Atlas, Archaeology, Aviation, Discovery, Family History, Fiction, History, Maritime, Military, Military Classics, Politics, Select, Transport, True Crime, Air World, Frontline Publishing, Leo Cooper, Remember When, Seaforth Publishing, The Praetorian Press, Wharncliffe Local History, Wharncliffe Transport, Wharncliffe True Crime and White Owl.

For a complete list of Pen & Sword titles please contact
PEN & SWORD BOOKS LIMITED
47 Church Street, Barnsley, South Yorkshire S70 2AS, England
E-mail: enquiries@pen-and-sword.co.uk
Website: www.pen-and-sword.co.uk

Contents

About the Author

Ian Baxter is a military historian who specialises in German twentieth-century military history. He has written more than fifty books including *Poland – The Eighteen Day Victory March*, *Panzers In North Africa*, *The Ardennes Offensive*, *The Western Campaign*, *The 12th SS Panzer-Division Hitlerjugend*, *The Waffen-SS on the Western Front*, *The Waffen-SS on the Eastern Front*, *The Red Army at Stalingrad*, *Elite German Forces of World War II*, *Armoured Warfare*, *German Tanks of War*, *Blitzkrieg*, *Panzer-Divisions at War*, *Hitler's Panzers*, *German Armoured Vehicles of World War Two*, *Last Two Years of the Waffen-SS at War*, *German Soldier Uniforms and Insignia*, *German Guns of the Third Reich*, *Defeat to Retreat: The Last Years of the German Army At War 1943–45*, *Operation Bagration – the Destruction of Army Group Centre*, *German Guns of the Third Reich*, *Rommel and the Afrika Korps*, *U-Boat War*, and most recently *The Sixth Army and the Road to Stalingrad*. He has written over a hundred articles including 'Last days of Hitler', 'Wolf's Lair', 'The Story of the V1 and V2 Rocket Programme', 'Secret Aircraft of World War Two', 'Rommel at Tobruk', 'Hitler's War With his Generals', 'Secret British Plans to Assassinate Hitler', 'The SS at Arnhem', 'Hitlerjugend', 'Battle of Caen 1944', 'Gebirgsjäger at War', 'Panzer Crews', 'Hitlerjugend Guerrillas', 'Last Battles in the East', 'The Battle of Berlin', and many more. He has also reviewed numerous military studies for publication, supplied thousands of photographs and important documents to various publishers and film production companies worldwide, and lectures to various schools, colleges and universities throughout the United Kingdom and the Republic of Ireland.

Introduction

This book is a record of German armour during operations in North Africa between 1941 and 19 43. Using rare and unpublished photographs, it represents a visual account of the various elements that went into making the *Deutsches Afrikakorps* (*Afrika Korps*, *Afrikakorps*, or DAK) a legendary army.

It reveals the different armoured vehicles that fought in Field-Marshal Erwin Rommel's force, ranging from the light, to the medium, to the deadly, heavy Panzers such as the Tiger. It shows the diverse armoured support, including self-propelled guns, armoured cars and personnel carriers, as well as field cars and motorcycles. It also reveals the different types of reconnaissance vehicles, and the halftracks that brought the troops to the front line of the battlefield. Among other subjects, it covers the heavy Tiger tank battalions and the *Sturmartillerie*, along with their fighting techniques. It traces the evolution of the *Afrika Korps* on the battlefield, from the deployment of the little *Panzerkampfwagen* I, right through to the Tiger.

With detailed captions and text the book tells the story of the infamous Panzer divisions that fought successfully across the desert against determined British and Commonwealth forces, and then how it battled in despair and defeat. During its two-year existence the *Deutsches Afrikakorps* achieved unequalled progress in the evolution of its armoured vehicles. Its deployment of tanks and support vehicles had been masterly, planned by the brilliant tactician Rommel, the 'Desert Fox'.

Chapter One

Desert Blitzkrieg 1941

On 3 February 1941, General Erwin Rommel, who had achieved great successes in France in 1940 with his 7th Panzer Division was chosen by Hitler to go to North Africa to 'explore the current situation'. The situation that Hitler referred to was the problems the Italian Army was experiencing against British Commonwealth troops under the command of General Richard O'Connor. By the end of January 1941, Mussolini had lost some 130,000 troops and 380 tanks. It was a major humiliation to the Italian dictator, who had been compelled to ask for help from Hitler or face complete annihilation in North Africa. To the Führer, the thought of sending German units to North Africa appealed greatly. The plan would not only restore the prestige of the Axis, but also consolidate the German strategic position in the desert against the British. Hitler was confident of victory.

On 12 February Rommel landed in North Africa with the Italian Army still in full retreat. Two days later, thousands of tonnes of equipment and supplies arrived, including the advanced units of the new *Afrika Korps* comprising the 5th Light and 3rd Panzer Regiments, as well as reconnaissance soldiers and support units. The force was put together from the second regiment of the 3rd Panzer Division, organized into the 5th Light Division, joined by elements of the 15th Panzer Division transferred from Italy.

German armour in North Africa consisted of various halftracks, reconnaissance vehicles, light and heavy armoured cars, and tanks. The Panzers employed for battle were mainly the Pz.Kpfw.I, II, III and IV, including the Czech Pz.Kpfw.35(t) and 38(t). Supporting these were the tank hunters or *Panzerjäger* which chiefly comprised a 4.7cm PaK (t) (Sf) or a 15cm sIG 33 (Sf) on a *Panzerkampfwagen* I.

In early March 1941, Rommel ordered General Johannes Streich's 5th Light Division to drive eastwards along the coast from Syrte in what was known as Operation Sonnenblume. By 4 March, Streich was optimistic about driving the British from their positions, and within days a number of Pz.Kpfw.Is, including Pz.Kpfw.35(t) and 38(t)s, supported by foot soldiers and artillery, managed to chase the enemy across the desert toward Mersa el Brega. It did not take long before the British were forced onto the retreat, abandoning their positions. The 5th Light Division continued its drive across the desert at breakneck speed, with British forces desperately trying to hold ground against tanks and charging German soldiers. Despite orders from Berlin to slow the advance, Rommel ignored the directives as he was determined not to allow the British to regroup and bring up more armour. Instead, the master tactician ordered a dramatic three-pronged assault to exploit the enemy's confusion. Supported by two Italian divisions, German armoured units attacked the defenders and drove them further back, forcing parts of the British force to withdraw from the peninsula of Cyrenaica. There followed a trail of destruction all the way to Benghazi.

The German drive across the desert was a dazzling display of tactical genius. Rommel's armour had exploited its foe using Blitzkrieg tactics that had been formulated in the flat plains of northern France and Belgium. However, in Berlin the news of the general's success was met with dismay. The German Army High Command were increasingly concerned that the Afrika Korps would overstretch its supplies, become outflanked, and then cut off.

Rommel, on the other hand, was more convinced than ever of success and believed the important strategic port of Tobruk would soon be taken. He was aware that Tobruk had to be captured before he could resume his offensive towards Egypt. The British garrison was determined that Tobruk was not going to be another Dunkirk. On 11 April the Germans attacked the British and Commonwealth fortress defending Tobruk. Defence was stiff and German units were repelled several times. In fact, resistance was so tough that Rommel angrily wired Berlin urgently requesting an airlift of the 15th Panzer Division. The first units of the 15th Panzer Division arrived a few days later, but further attacks against the Tobruk garrison still failed. Fighting continued to rage on both sides, and there were no signs that the enemy would be driven from the port. Rommel, frustrated and irritable, formed a bold plan to swing his armour around Tobruk and drive the bulk of his force towards Sollum. What followed outside Sollum in the scorching heat and choking dust was a bloody and violent tank and infantry battle that saw the German and Italian attackers win a much-needed victory.

Late in the summer of 1941, the *Afrika Korps* was renamed *Panzergruppe Afrika* and was strengthened and upgraded. It now boasted six Italian divisions and included the *Afrika Korps* 15th and 21st Panzer Divisions and the 90th Light Division which included old units of the 5th Light Division.

Rommel's force was now much stronger than it had been when it first arrived in Africa. The general was determined more than ever to reach the Egyptian border and destroy the British there. He was also eager to take the garrison at Tobruk, which was still resisting. The British had been continually reinforcing its army and to prevent this Rommel ordered some of his heavier tank units to block a corridor through to Tobruk. There followed a tank battle across fifty square miles of desert to the west of the garrison in which Pz.Kpfw.IIIs and IVs, despite being outnumbered, demonstrated a mastery of mobile operations, with tactical opportunism and enthusiasm. In fact, many of the junior tank commanders actually learnt their trade in the desert, and a number of them went on to command successfully in other theatres of operation in both Europe and Russia.

First they outflanked, encircled and destroyed many units. Then they sped towards the Halfaya Pass and Sidi Omar. However, British lines once again strengthened and, with further reinforcements, now began advancing towards Rommel's over-stretched lines. Almost out of fuel, ammunition and reserves, advanced elements of *Panzergruppe Afrika* were ordered immediately to swing round and withdraw from Cyrenaica. This included dismantling the siege apparatus east of Tobruk. On Christmas day, Benghazi fell into British hands and by the end of 1941 *Panzergruppe* was back where it had started.

A Pz.Kpfw.III being carefully unloaded from a transport ship onto the dockside. This tank was primarily designed to fight other tanks. Initially designers urged that the 5cm gun be specified on all these variants. However, the infantry in early 1941 were still being equipped with the 3.7cm PaK 35/36, and it was thought that in the interest of standardisation the Pz.Kpfw.III should carry the same armament, much to the detriment of the crews.

(**Above**) Another Pz.Kpfw.III being unloaded from a transport ship. The primary task of the Pz.Kpfw.III was to fight other tanks. But although it was a well-built tank, in terms of armour, armament and mobility, it was not outstanding. However, in North Africa it proved its worth and was highly successful. Note the 20-litre jerry cans onboard the vehicle to sustain the vast distances in which these vehicles had to advance on a daily basis.

(**Opposite, above**) A Pz.Kpfw.II being suspended over the dockside during the unloading of German armour for the North African campaign. All production variants of the Pz.Kpfw.II were fitted with the 140PS, gasoline-fuelled six-cylinder Maybach HL 62 TRM engine and ZF transmissions. The Ausf.A, B and C variants had a top speed of 25mph, while the Ausf.D and E had a torsion bar suspension and a much superior transmission giving a top road speed 33mph. However, across country where this vehicle would be used mainly, it had a much lower speed than previous models. The F variant was replaced with the old leaf-spring type suspension making it much faster. The Pz.Kpfw.II had a three-man crew. The driver sat in the forward hull, while the commander sat in a turret seat and was also the gunner. The radio operator was positioned on the floor of the tank under the turret.

(**Opposite, below**) A Pz.Kpfw.III at the dockside. Its tactical number is simply marked with a white three-digit number '221' on either side of the turret and has been painted. The vehicle has a base pattern of *Grünbraun* RAL 8000 with a one-third disruptive overspray of RAL 7008 *Graugrün* (also known as *Khakibraun*). This camouflage scheme was painted on the majority of armoured vehicles in North Africa until April 1942. Following that, the base colour was altered to RAL 8020 *Gelbbraun* with one-third disruptive overspray of RAL 7027 *Sandgrau*.

(**Above**) A Pz.Kpfw.III displaying its tactical number '134' marked in white over the vehicle's base pattern of *Grünbraun* RAL 8000 with a 1/3 disruptive overspray of RAL 7008 *Graugrün*. The Panzer III Ausf.A through C were powered by a 250PS (184 kW) 12-cylinder Maybach HL 108 TR engine giving a top speed of 32km/h and a range of 150km (93 miles).

(**Opposite, above**) A column of Pz.Kpfw.IVs advance along a road in Tripoli, clearly displaying their power to the local inhabitants. The Pz.Kpfw.IV became the most popular Panzer of the war and remained in production throughout. At first it was not intended to be the main armoured vehicle of the *Panzerwaffe*, but it soon proved to be so diverse and effective that it became the most widely used of all the main battle tanks during the conflict. During 1941 and 1942 the Pz.Kpfw.IV fought with distinction in North Africa, and supported the infantry extensively throughout.

(**Opposite, below**) An Sd.Kfz.263 leads an armoured column along the sea front in Tripoli. The Sd.Kfz.263 was a radio vehicle equipped with a long range radio set with its telescoping mast antennas. It was also equipped with the MG 34 machine gun. In France in 1940 it had proved to be a dependable armoured car able to defend itself from localized attack. These vehicles could still move even after enemy fire had damaged one or more wheels. In the desert, the armoured cars and armoured personnel carriers of the reconnaissance battalions provided the mobility that was pivotal to the success for Blitzkrieg. Great importance too had been placed upon their quality of firepower, protection, and flexibility with the main objective of collating and sending back important battlefield intelligence.

(**Above**) A Kübelwagen armoured car leads a column of vehicles through Tripoli in April 1941. Crowds of people can be seen standing at the roadside watching the spectacle.

(**Opposite, above**) A column of Pz.Kpfw.IIIs advance through Tripoli in early 1941. The Pz.Kpfw.III variants A through to C had 15mm homogeneous steel armour on all sides with 10mm on top and 5mm on the bottom. During the early part of the war tank commanders knew that this new Panzer would be well protected against their lightly armed opponents. It moved out onto the battlefield with the sole intention of fighting with other tanks. It was initially equipped with the 3.7cm KwK 36 L/46.5 cannon, which proved more than adequate against British armour. However, the tank was later up-armoured with the short barrelled 5cm KwK 38 L/42 gun.

(**Opposite, below**) A photograph taken showing Rommel's Tripoli headquarters in 1941. When Rommel arrived in North Africa he wasted no time to start planning the for the *Afrika Korps* attacks against British and Commonwealth forces in the desert.

A member of headquarters staff is seen here seen marking final corrections to Rommel's plans before the *Afrika Korps* attacked in the desert.

Rommel can be seen in discussion with an Italian general walking along a road in Tripoli. When Rommel arrived in Tripoli the Italian army were on the brink of destruction. The general immediately visited the Italian General Garibaldi to discuss the dire situation and the battle plan.

Pictured intently outlining plans using a pencil on a map table, General Rommel can be seen plotting his first attacks against his enemy. Behind him transport ships can be seen in the bay outside Tripoli in early 1941.

Two crew members stand next to their Pz.Kpfw.II out in the Libyan desert in 1941. The vehicle is painted with a base pattern of *Grünbraun* RAL 8000 with a 1/3 disruptive overspray of RAL 7008 *Graugrün*. The tactical number 432 is painted in a white outline.

Operating along the coast, an Sd.Kfz.231 can be seen. It is armed with the 2cm KwK 30 or 38 and one coaxial MG 34 machine gun. These heavy reconnaissance vehicles were found extensively in the desert in the heavy detachment of the Aufkl.Abt of motorized infantry and Panzer divisions to provide direct support for the lighter armoured cars.

(**Opposite, above**) Two Pz.Kpfw.IVs out in the desert. Most of the armoured vehicles were given an application of tropical camouflage, with the widespread use of sand colour schemes, yellow-brown RAL 8000, grey-green RAL 7008, or just brown RAL 8017. In this photograph these Panzers are finished in over-all yellow-brown RAL 8000. The nearest tank carries a large number '4' painted in red with a white outline on the turret sides.

(**Opposite, below**) A *Schwerer Panzerspähwagen* Sd.Kfz.231 during operations in 1941. This reconnaissance vehicle is fitted with the cast visors on the turret which were introduced around 1939, and has an armoured cowl on the rear to the protect the radiator. This eight-wheeled vehicle could be driven at the same speed both in reverse and forward, thanks to a transmission with six forward and six reverse gears. It is armed with the 2cm KwK 30 or 38 and one coaxial MG 34. They were issued to the heavy detachment of the Aufkl.Abt of motorized infantry and panzer divisions to provide support for lighter armoured cars. They were produced from 1936 until May 1942, but the Sd.Kfz.232 radio version was built until September 1943.

(**Opposite, above**) An *Afrika Korps* crew of an Sd.Kfz.231 can be seen sitting on their vehicle while one of the crew members plays an accordion. It is armed with the 2cm KwK 30 and an MG 34 for local fire support. The 231 was introduced into service in 1932 and began to be replaced in 1937 when the *Wehrmacht* began producing eight-wheeled armoured vehicles instead of six-wheeled. The crew comprised the commander, gunner, driver, and a radio operator/rear driver. The vehicle is being transported on a special flatbed rail car to another part of the front.

(**Opposite, below**) Pz.Kpfw.IIs on the advance. Although this Panzer had originally been designed as a stopgap while larger, more advanced tanks were developed, it still played an important role in North Africa. This light tank had a three-man crew with the driver sitting in the forward left hull with the gearbox on the right. The commander sat in a seat in the turret and was tasked with firing the cannon and co-axial machine gun, while the loader/radio operator sat on the floor plates of the tank behind the driver. He had a radio on the left and a number of 2cm ammunition storage bins.

(**Above**) Two Pz.Kpfw.IIIs can be seen crossing the desert. A distinct feature of this tank was a three-man turret. This meant that the commander was not distracted by either the loader or gunner and could fully concentrate on his own tasks.

(**Above**) A *Sonderkraftfahrzeug* Sd.Kfz.250 halftrack. This halftrack was designed to deliver armoured reconnaissance troops to the Panzer and Panzergrenadier divisions with a flexible armoured vehicle that possessed better off-road capability than the Sd.Kfz.222 armoured cars. It was also used as a platoon and company commander's vehicle. The command vehicle was equipped with various decoding and deciphering apparatus and a variety of radios and antenna. It was armed with either one or two MG 34s on pivot mounts and could carry a crew of six. In this photograph two men can be seen surveying the terrain ahead using 6 × 30 binoculars. Note the national flag for aerial recognition draped over the front of the vehicle's engine compartment.

(**Opposite, above**) A photograph showing later production Sd.Kfz.231 that was used during the campaign in North Africa. The shape of the rear plates was modified by an armoured cowl installed on the rear to protect the radiator. Initially this vehicle was not fitted with a radio but was later modified to carry one as can be seen by the antenna mounted on the turret.

(**Opposite, below**) A soldier stands next to his Sd.Kfz.8 prime mover out in the open desert. The halftrack is towing a 15cm heavy howitzer. These vehicles were seen extensively operating in North Africa. Some 4,000 of them were built during the Second World War.

(**Opposite, above**) A column of Pz.Kpfw.Is. This light Panzer featured a two-man crew comprising a driver and a commander; the latter was also used as the gunner. The driver sat in the forward hull of the cramped vehicle on the left, while the commander occupied the turret to the right. The tank was armed with two 7.92mm machine guns, both of which were capable of firing 650 rounds per minute. They could only be traversed by the commander by hand. Entry and exit for the commander was through the small turret roof, while the driver could exit or enter the vehicle by a hinged rectangular door on the left of the superstructure. The tank had minimal armoured protection and featured five road wheels to a track side and each wheel was encased in rubber. Three rollers were fitted to the underside of the upper track run. Operating weight was listed at 5.9 tons and power came from a single Krupp M 305 air-cooled, four-cylinder petrol engine delivering up to sixty horsepower. The Ausf.A could manage a top road speed of 23mph, with an operational range of 85 miles cross country or 125 miles on road.

(**Above**) A Pz.Kpfw.II has been chocked and chained onto a flatbed vehicle destined for North Africa in 1941. The vehicle is finished in yellow brown RAL 8000 and carries the number '143' painted in a white outline on the turret sides. Note the *Afrika Korps* palm tree insignia painted in yellow.

(**Opposite, below**) A Horch field staff car leading an Sd.Kfz.263 followed by two Sd.Kfz.221 or 223 light armoured cars. The vehicle is clearly displaying the *Afrika Korps* palm tree insignia on the left fender. On the other fender it displays the white tactical sign for a reconnaissance unit.

(**Opposite, above**) A number of armoured vehicles on the advance are spread out. They comprise mainly Pz.Kpfw.II, III and IV. Rommel adopted Blitzkrieg tactics in North Africa where an attacking force spearheaded with the use of concentrated armour and motorised infantry formations supported by aerial attacks. The attacks were fast and powerful, often using speed as a surprise and encircling the enemy in the process. Through the employment of manoeuvre using armour, Blitzkrieg made it difficult for the enemy to respond due to the front constantly changing. With enemy encircled, it could be concentrated and destroyed.

(**Opposite, below**) An Sd.Kfz.7 halftrack has halted in the desert pulling an 8.8cm FlaK 18 on a Sd.Ah 201 limber. The vehicle has rod style grab handles mounted between the row of seats in order to allow quick mounting and dismounting by the crew. One of the limber tyres is being replaced by the crew.

(**Above**) Resting infantry rise to their feet as a Funkpanzerwagen Sd.Kfz.251/3 Ausf.C containing General Erwin Rommel passes by. In the distance smoke rises in the air following heavy fighting. This halftrack is a command vehicle and fitted with the standard long range antenna.

An Sd.Kfz.8 prime mover advancing across the desert with a full complement of troop personnel. These special motorised halftrack vehicles saw widespread use in North Africa. Its main roles were for the towing of heavy ordnance such as the 21cm Mörser, the 15cm FlaK 18 and the 10.5cm FlaK 38. However, it also served as an infantry transport, as in this photograph.

Pz.Kpfw.IIs role along a road in the summer of 1941. Although these vehicles were under-gunned and under-armoured they still managed to fight with success on the battlefield. However, by late the following year, the majority of Pz.Kpfw.IIs were withdrawn from the front and performed scouting missions instead.

Pz.Kpfw.Is and Pz.Kpfw.IIs with full provisions have been unloaded at the dockside in Tripoli, and the crews can be seen preparing their machines. The vehicles, of the 5th Light Division, retain their 1940 dark grey camouflage paint. They arrived in Libya still displaying the 3rd Panzer Division markings in yellow, as can be identified by the inverted 'Y' and two marks painted on the rear of the tanks' offside fenders.

Photographed from a vehicle, Pz.Kpfw.IVs can be seen on the move during an operation in the summer of 1941. Throughout the North African campaign the Pz.Kpfw.IV fought with distinction.

(**Opposite, above**) M13/40 Italian tanks can be seen spread out in the desert in 1941. The M13/40 weighed some thirteen tons and was armed with a 47mm gun with armour-piercing capability. The tank had a four-men crew and was used throughout the war. Note the turret hatches are open in an attempt by the crew to cool the inside of the tank. For safety's sake hatches were normally closed down if the enemy was in close proximity. The crew would then sweat and choke, sometimes for hours, as the vehicle's air filters would often become clogged as they crossed the dusty and sandy terrain.

(**Opposite, below**) An interesting photograph showing a Pz.Kpfw.III set up as a command post in the middle of the desert. Tarpaulin has been used to protect the crew against the dust and sun, and a radio antenna has been erected. Note the washing line.

(**Above**) An Sd.Kfz.7 hauling an 8.8cm FlaK gun has halted in the desert. The crew are preparing to unlimber the gun and bring it into action against enemy targets. The 8.8cm FlaK was a deadly and effective piece of weaponry and scored sizable hits both in an anti-aircraft role and against ground targets as well. The guns served well during the North African campaign and scored considerable success owing to the rapid transportation of the weapon to the front lines.

(**Above**) A Pz.Kpfw.III can be seen halted in a town. The vehicle is full of provisions for the considerable distances it had to travel across the desert.

(**Opposite, above**) *Afrika Korps* troops survey a British Morris C8 4 × 4 quad field artillery tractor that has attempted to cross a trench and become stuck. The crew more than likely bailed out and abandoned it.

(**Opposite, below**) An interesting photograph showing what appears to be a Pz.Kpfw.IV Ausf.E out in the desert. The canvas tent erected next to it is one of the covers the British used to disguise their tanks from the air as transport trucks. The Panzer is from Panzer Regiment 8 of the 15th Panzer Division. Note the tank's pivoting driver's visor from a Pz.Kpfw.III Ausf.G.

(**Above**) A light Horch cross-country vehicle moves across the desert. The vehicle's canopy can be seen raised to reduce the sun's rays penetrating down on the driver and passengers, and to prevent hot dust particles entering the cabin.

(**Opposite, above**) An Sd.Kfz.263 on the move. This vehicle was issued to the *Nachrichten Abteilung* of the motorized infantry and Panzer divisions as well as corps and army headquarters. This radio vehicle or *Funkspähwagen* was equipped with long-range radio equipment and an additional radio operator. It was large but fast and a versatile addition to ground forces before and during the early war period. To support the long wave radio equipment the turret was omitted, the superstructure was raised and only a single ball-mounted machine gun was mounted.

(**Opposite, below**) *Afrika Korps* troops captured many Commonwealth vehicles. Here infantry have captured and are looting a British Marmon-Harrington that has been adapted on rails.

(**Above**) A FlaK gunner poses for the camera on board his Sd.Kfz.10. This halftrack was primarily built for towing medium to light ordinance and trailers. It was also adapted to mount the 2cm FlaK 30. The special platform was built with fold-down side and rear panels that gave the crew additional space during combat.

(**Opposite, above**) In this photograph an Opel Maultier is towing a 10.5cm Le.FH 18 leaving the nose ramp of a Messerschmitt 323 'Gigant' transport plane. By mid-1941 most supplies were being transported by air.

(**Opposite, below**) Out in the field and the crew can be seen relaxing next to their Pz.Kpfw.III Ausf.G. Two of the men are wearing the distinctive *Afrika Korps* pith helmet which was widely worn among the infantry during the early part of the campaign. The Ausf.G variant was initially very similar to the Ausf.F. The first fifty were built with the 3.7cm gun while the remaining 550 used the 5cm gun, as pictured in this photograph. The rear armour of the Ausf.G had been increased to 30mm, and a pivoting visor was added for the driver.

A Panzerjäger I can be seen on the advance. These vehicles were the first fully-tracked self-propelled anti-tank guns in German service and were created by mounting a well-designed ex-Czech 4.7cm PaK(t) on a modified Pz.Kpfw.I Ausf.B chassis. While they performed with success during the French and Balkan campaigns, in North Africa the vehicle was underpowered and the gun had limited capabilities to counter lager Commonwealth tanks.

A Pz.Kpfw.IV Ausf.F1 on the move across the desert in mid-1941. This modified variant's armoured plating was increased. Its front bow plate appliqué was changed to a full 50mm thick armoured plate. Side armour and turret thickness was raised to 30mm. Other modifications were larger track links from 380mm to 400mm to reduce ground pressure, and both the idler wheel and front drive sprockets were modified.

An Sd.Kfz.251 halted in the desert with a variety of other vehicles including a Pz.Kpfw.III and an Sd.Kfz.232 (8-rad) radio vehicle. This radio vehicle was equipped with a long-range radio set and usually found in signals units.

Chapter Two

Attack and Retreat 1942

Although the *Afrika Korps* had retreated across nearly 300 miles of desert, Rommel's armour had withdrawn without serious loss. During the first weeks of January 1942 his force was resupplied, rested and reorganized. On 21 January, he sent his tanks back into action. Almost immediately the *Afrika Korps* outwitted, outmanoeuvred and outgunned their enemy. Within five days they had knocked out 299 enemy tanks and armoured fighting vehicles and 147 guns. The British were now in full retreat and Benghazi was retaken. In just two weeks Rommel's Panzers had bulldozed halfway back across Cyrenaica with the intention of capturing Tobruk and advancing on Egypt and the Nile.

In April, Rommel secretly reshuffled his Panzer army to prepare them for an attack on the British Gazala Line, which ran down from the coast into the desert forty miles west of Tobruk. He planned to outwit the British by sending his entire force across the desert in a bold outflanking move round the southern end of the Gazala Line; then he intended to drive north to capture Tobruk.

On 26 May the offensive began, with 10,000 vehicles moving south. Chaos followed, as the British were ready. They attacked in force and destroyed much of Rommel's armour.

However, the *Afrika Korps* remained undaunted and pushed forward towards Bir Hakeim. Rommel ordered his tanks to wheel northwards in sweeping outflanking moves through the disintegrating Gazala Line towards Tobruk. Gazala fell on 5 June and two weeks later the 21st Panzer along with 90th Light Division and 15th Panzer Division broke through the Tobruk perimeter capturing some 35,000 prisoners.

The British Eight Army were forced to withdraw and it seemed victory beckoned for Rommel. But his panzer force had taken a severe battering and by the end of June were only able to field forty-four tanks between the 15th and 21st Panzer Division. Most of the transport vehicles too had been captured or destroyed.

Despite the losses, the Germans continued and tore into the British defences at Mersa Matruh. The 21st Panzer Division soon became engaged in an intense armoured battled with the 2nd New Zealand Division in what became known as the

Battle of Mersa Matruh. Fighting was heavy but German firepower and tactics prevailed and saw the enemy withdraw to a new line at El Alamein.

By July the German striking force was only 62 miles from the great British naval base at Alexandria. It now seemed that Rommel would be victorious. However, the British Eighth Army was strong, and in spite of a series of ferocious German attacks the Afrika Korps was halted during the first Battle of El Alamein. For weeks fighting continued to rage and at the end of August Rommel made a last-ditch effort to capture positions during the Battle of Alam el Halfa. Once again the Germans were repulsed. Fighting was severe and the commander of the 21st Panzer Division, General Georg Von Bismarck, was killed by a British mine. Major General Carl Hans Lungerhausen took over temporary command until Major General Heinz von Randow arrived on 18 September.

On 23 October, the British offensive and the Second Battle of El Alamein was unleashed. For the battle Rommel decided that he wanted to avoid his normal tactics of moving his reserve armoured strength in a single concentrated attack. Instead he divided them into a northern group consisting of the 15th Panzer and Littorio Divison, and a southern group consisting of the 21st Panzer and Ariete Division. Both were organised into battle groups, *Kampfgruppe*, and were employed further forward than normal. The 15th Panzer Division had 125 tanks comprising 16 Pz.Kpfw.IIs, 43 Pz.Kpfw.III *Ausführung* H, 43 Pz.Kpfw.III Ausf.J, 6 Pz.Kpfw.IV Ausf.D, and 15 Pz.kpfw IV Ausf.F, while the 21st Panzer Division had 121 tanks consisting of 12 Pz.Kpfw.IIs, 38 Pz.Kpfw.III Ausf.H, 43 Pz.Kpfw.III Ausf.J, 2 Pz.Kpfw.IV Ausf.D, and 15 Pz.Kpwf IV Ausf.F. Behind these tanks the 90th Light and Trieste Motorised Divisions were held in reserve near the coast.

Although low on fuel, Rommel's force surged forward against strong British resistance. Over the next few days fighting raged and the *Afrika Korps* took massive losses. With Rommel struggling to keep his force together and trying to avert destruction, Hitler sent him a message:

> To Field Marshal Rommel. It is with trusting confidence in your leadership and the courage of the German-Italian troops under your command that the German people and I are following the heroic struggle in Egypt. In the situation which you find yourself there can be no other thought but to stand fast, yield not a yard of ground and throw every gun and every man into the battle. Considerable air force reinforcements are being sent to C-in-C North Africa. The Duce and the Commando Supremo are also making the utmost efforts to send you the means to continue the fight. Your enemy, despite his superiority, must also be at the end of his strength. It would not be the first time in history that a strong will has triumphed over the bigger battalions. As to your troops, you can show them no other road than that to victory or death. Adolf Hitler.

In spite of this message, nothing could stop the impending slaughter. The Trento Division lost half its infantry and virtually all its artillery, the 164th Light Division lost two battalions, and although the 15th Panzer Division and the Littorio Divisions had gallantly beaten off constant Allied attacks, this had come at a heavy price: the 15th Panzer Division had only thirty-one tanks left, and the other units were under strength and lacked supplies. The 21st Panzer Division found itself overwhelmed by British artillery and tanks and by the end of October was reduced to just four tanks.

The situation was grim for the *Afrika Korps*. They had failed to capture Tobruk or El Alamein and were no longer able to hold positions. With lack of armour, supplies, soldiers and fuel, Rommel was compelled to undergo a long and painful retreat to Tunisia. He instructed the battle-bruised 21st Panzer Division to fight rearguard actions as the main force retreated across the desert.

To make matters worse, on 8 November news reached Rommel's command vehicle that the Anglo-Americans had landed in Morocco and Algeria during what was called Operation Torch. *Panzerarmee Afrika* were now threatened with annihilation. German and Italian forces made a fighting withdrawal to El Agheila with Rommel conducting a textbook retreat, destroying all equipment left behind and planting the land behind him with mines and booby traps.

Afrika Korps troops come across an abandoned British Grant tank. These tanks served with the British in North Africa until the end of the campaign. The M3 was able to engage German tanks and towed anti-tank guns. Its high silhouette and low, hull-mounted 75mm cannon were drawbacks, since they prevented fighting from a hull-down firing position.

Officers in the field rest on Italian deckchairs liberated from a Libyan beach in 1942.

(**Above**) *Afrika Korps* soldiers examine an abandoned British Matilda tank. With its heavy armour, the Matilda was an excellent infantry support tank, but with relatively limited speed and armament. It was used extensively against German armour in North Africa and was the only British tank to serve from the start of the war to its end.

(**Opposite, above**) An assorted group of *Afrika Korps* officers around their commander in the field during operations in early 1942. A variety of uniform styles existed in the ranks of the German army in North Africa, but the bleaching effects of the heat, sun and desert air changed their colours and made them all look dirty and difficult to distinguish.

(**Opposite, below**) In an outpost these officers can be seen conferring with the aid of maps.

Rommel conferring with two of his staff. Behind them is a halted Pz.Kpfw.III. Both the men are wearing greatcoats and carrying German army issue torches. Rommel, known as the 'Desert Fox', is wearing his famous looted British goggles. Behind them the curious crewmember of a Pz.Kpfw.III peers through the one-piece entry hatch on the turret side.

Two photographs taken in sequence showing Rommel conferring with his commanding officer.

With the aid of a map, Rommel is directing the movements of his Panzer force prior to an attack with one of his commanding officers.

Rommel can just be seen behind one of his commanding officers inside a light Horch cross-country vehicle that has halted. From inside the car the officer instructs his men.

Rommel confers with one of his staff from inside his light Horch cross-country vehicle. In the desert Rommel was often seen standing in his command car giving out orders and directing the campaign.

Another photograph, shot in sequence to the previous image, showing Rommel with personnel surveying the endless terrain using a map. Behind Rommel is a group of Italian officers. The Desert Fox had little time for Italian senior officers but had a paternal way with the Italian soldiers.

(**Opposite, above**) From Rommel's staff vehicle one of his Italian commanders can be seen standing up surveying the terrain through a pair of 6 × 30 binoculars.

(**Opposite, below**) Rommel seen in his staff car drinking coffee with one of his staff officers. The Desert Fox believed that his Panzer force should be led from the front, or as he said, 'from the saddle'.

(**Above**) Rommel seen conferring with an Italian general. Although there were language problems, the Desert Fox's drive and energy had helped turn around the Italian army's low morale.

Two photographs taken in sequence showing Rommel conferring with one of his commanders, in Tripoli.

Rommel inside a Kfz.15 mE medium standard passenger vehicle during operations at El Alamein. The vehicle's canopy has been raised to reduce the searing day-time temperatures and prevent dust from penetrating the vehicle.

Rommel, with his personal German and Italian staff, surveys the endless terrain ahead. Note the commander to Rommel's right wearing the famous *Afrika Korps* cuff band sewn onto his greatcoat. Behind the Desert Fox is a group of Italian officers.

(**Opposite, above**) Accompanied by his staff, in tropical uniform, Rommel salutes as he carries on with his mammoth task of defeating the British and Commonwealth forces.

(**Opposite, below**) A famous image of Rommel conferring with German and Italian commanders in the field. Between 1941 and 1942 Rommel showed a dogged determination to smash his opponents. On the battlefield again and again he showed all the hallmarks of a great commander by constantly outwitting, outmanoeuvring and outgunning his enemy.

(**Above**) Rommel walking along a street path in Tripoli conversing with two commanders.

Three photographs showing Rommel in his most comfortable position on the battlefield – leading his men and armour from the front. Often the Desert Fox was seen bucketing across the desert in his command vehicle, screaming out orders to prevent the rout and keeping his armoured forces moving at full speed. He allowed his men only minimal rest during the fighting, and this brought him many victories. Rommel was able to outmanoeuvre, overwhelm, and outfight the Allies, and nearly succeeded in destroying the British 8th Army. In June 1942 he pursued his defeated enemy to Tobruk, which he finally captured on 21 June. The next day the General was flown back to Hitler's East Prussian headquarters, the Wolfschanze, and the Führer promoted him to field marshal.

Inside an aircraft hangar Rommel can be seen speaking to Italian officers.

Wearing a life jacket, Rommel is about to fly back to Italy.

A Panzer *Oberstleutnant* from the 8th Panzer Regiment. Of interest, he does not wear the typical skulls of the Imperial German Hussars on his lapels. Note his Italian colonial helmet and silver tank battle badge.

A typical uniform of an *Afrika Korps* officer in the desert in 1942.

(**Opposite, above**) An Oberstleutnant from the 8th Panzer Regiment pictured on the left of the photograph confers with his commanders. Even *Afrika Korps* generals wore simplified olive-green dress in the desert.

(**Opposite, below**) Officers of the Corpo d'Armata Motorizzato (Motorized Army Corps) are seen here in the desert caked in dust. They are all wearing grey-green greatcoats. Note the Italian officer on the right wearing a British khaki side cap.

(**Above**) This photograph clearly shows the difference between obsolete Italian desert dress and the modern German desert uniforms. Pictured here are a group of Italian officers wearing Italian cork helmets with brass badges attached to the front. They are with a German commander.

(**Opposite, above**) On the left is Generalleutnant Crüwell, commander of the Afrika-Korps, in March 1942. He is pictured here wearing an M1940 tropical greatcoat. On the right the officer wears the M1940 motorcycle greatcoat in olive rubberised canvas. Note on the far right of the photograph is a wounded officer with a bandaged head under his field cap.

(**Opposite, below**) What appear to be Pz.Kpfw.IIIs ploughing through the open desert. Normally a battalion of tanks used a V formation, with two companies leading and one in reserve. These companies in line, with tanks in column, were normally in 55-metre intervals and advanced in waves across the desert.

(**Opposite, above**) Belonging to the 5th Panzer Regiment of the 5th Panzer Division these reconnaissance vehicles can be seen halted in the desert. On the left is an Sd.Kfz.223. Behind it is a Volkswagen Type 82 166 Kfz.1 cross-country light personnel carrier. The third vehicle is an early production Sd.Kfz.263 radio vehicle.

(**Opposite, below**) A Sd.Kfz.251 halftrack. Of interest is the MG 34 mounted on top which has been wrapped in canvas material to protect it from the desert sand. The vehicle carries a hood and, like most *Afrika Korps* vehicles, is more than likely carrying the white transverse air recognition stripe. Note that the halftrack carries the divisional command pennant to denote the presence of an officer. When the officer was not on board the pennants were removed or covered.

(**Above**) A Pz.Kpfw.IV has halted in the desert and the crew pose for the camera. The *Afrika Korps* only started receiving the Pz.Kpfw.IV with its longer, punchier L/48 cannon in small numbers at the end of August 1942. These vehicles were sent to North Africa equipped with additional tropical filters and improved ventilation system.

(**Opposite**) Two photographs showing an immediate supply base in the middle of the desert. These supply lines were the main artery to any army wishing to sustain itself in North Africa. By August 1942, due to the severity of RAF bombing attacks, German supplies were reduced by 20 per cent. Supply problems were further multiplied by the lack of spare parts for numerous vehicles. In fact, logistical problems had become dire and as a consequence armoured vehicles often only had enough fuel for three days of travel.

(**Above**) The crew of a Sd.Kfz.251 and a Pz.Kpfw.III Ausf.G survey the terrain. The halftrack has a spare wheel attached to its front, for additional armoured protection. The Panzer has also been given armoured protection by track link bolted to the armour plate front and sides. The Ausf.G is identifiable by the bolt flange around the mantlet and machine gun ball mount to which the waterproof fabric cover is attached.

Troops from the 5th Panzer Regiment can be seen with an Sd.Kfz.251 on the right and a Pz.Kpfw.III on the left. The Panzer is carrying a large box on the engine deck, more than likely containing supplies and tools.

Captured British soldiers can be seen inside an Sd.Kfz.251 halftrack. German armoured troops from the 8th Panzer Regiment can be seen with the PoWs.

A Pz.Kpfw.III Ausf.G on the advance supporting infantry as they move across the desert during operations in the summer of 1942. The Panzer has additional track links bolted to the front of the vehicle including spare road wheels for armoured protection. Note the two pith helmets attached to the turret sides.

Another two Pz.Kpfw.III Ausf.Gs on the advance. The 5cm KwK 39 L/60 cannon was capable of penetrating most Allied tanks used in Africa, and until more long-barrelled Pz.Kpfw.IVs were available in numbers, the Pz.Kpfw.III had to bear the brunt of the anti-tank fighting in the Panzer divisions.

A command Pz.Bef.Wg.III on the move with what appears to be a captured Allied vehicle following behind in the distance. Note the *Rahmenantenne* or frame antenna on the engine deck.

A Pz.Kpfw.III passes a destroyed vehicle in the desert. This vehicle is armed with the 5cm KwK L/42 cannon. In Africa the Pz.Kpfw.III constituted the backbone of Rommel's armoured forces against British tanks.

A column of armoured vehicles on the advance along a road. The near tank in the photograph can be recognised as being a Pz.Kpfw.II Ausf.L and is identified by the spaced armour plate on the gun mantle, which can be seen protruding past the forward edge of the turret side plate.

A column of Pz.Kpfw.IIIs negotiate a British defensive position, passing concrete tank obstacles. The Pz.Kpfw.III fought well in the desert where speed combined with the tactical genius of Rommel proved invaluable.

(**Opposite, above**) At a command post is an Sd.Kfz.251 with radio antennae and mast. This photograph was taken in June 1942. Of interest, note the vast array of vehicles spread out across the desert. In mid-June the 21st Panzer along with 90th Light Division and 15th Panzer Division broke through the Tobruk perimeter capturing some 35,000 prisoners.

(**Opposite, below**) An Sd.Kfz.10 hauls a 35/36 3.7cm PaK gun. Note the 20-litre jerry cans on board the halftrack. The removable side body panels are in place and the tractor is piled high with the crew's necessities for desert combat.

(**Above**) A Pz.Kpfw.III Ausf.G belonging to the 21st Panzer Division. The basic tank regiment had altered three times between the start of the campaign in February 1941 and mid-1942. Each was supposed to contain some 204 Panzer, of which 136 were light armoured combat vehicles. By mid-1942 these numbers were never reached due to losses and supply difficulties.

(**Above**) A Pz.Kpfw.III racing across the desert. Panzer tactics, those particularly employed by Pz.Kpfw.III crews, usually began with opening fire about 1,600 metres, which was normally beyond the effective range of enemy weapons.

(**Opposite, above**) Climbing a sand dune is a Pz.Kpfw.III. Of interest, several stick grenades can be seen mounted on the turret sides. Water bottles are attached to the rear turret. The crew have stored numerous items over the engine deck, including a stowage box full of supplies and rolled-up canvas sheeting.

(**Opposite, below**) A variety of armoured vehicles and tanks are seen during an offensive operation in the desert. These vehicles are using the famous *Afrika Korps* V formation. The Panzers often used this formation moving in short wide sweeping rushes, taking full advantage of the wide-open terrain. Despite the rapid advance of these vehicles, field artillery and anti-tank weapons were kept as close as possible.

(**Opposite, above**) A column of Pz.Kpfw.IIIs from the 15th Panzer Division advance along a road bound for Tilimun Soluch.

(**Above**) A Funkpanzerwagen Sd.Kfz.251 radio command vehicle advancing through the desert. In North Africa the Sd.Kfz.251 halftrack was supplied in limited numbers, as only two Panzer divisions were employed. There were no real tropicalised versions, only late variants in the field.

(**Opposite, below**) Tank crews owed much of their success to their well-appointed maintenance companies which kept the vehicles in fighting condition. Heavier armour such as the Pz.Kpfw.IV and later the Tiger tanks made it more resistant to combat failure, and after quick repairs they could be returned to combat. Lighter tanks needed more time for repairs, especially if they were damaged, and often had to be transferred to specialised workshops.

(**Opposite, above**) A column of Pz.Kpfw.IIIs have halted at the side of the road during operations in 1942. The vehicle leading the column is an Ausf.J. The first version of the Ausf.J saw the frontal armour on the hull and superstructure and the rear hull armour increased in thickness from 30mm to 50mm. Hitler had ordered the use of the longer 50cm KwK 39 L/60, but 1,500 tanks had been produced using the short gun before that order was implemented.

(**Opposite, below**) Through the desert and a long column of armoured vehicles can be seen halted on a road as an 8.8cm FlaK gun crew limber up their weapon. The '88' could actually be fired while mounted on its limbers, but the instability affected the accuracy and the rate of fire. Although the 8.8cm FlaK gun was widely used as an anti-tank gun it also possessed a genuine anti-tank capability. On the battlefield it proved a very versatile weapon and continued being used in a dual role until the end of the war. The 8.8cm FlaK gun was used in the desert where they were prominently positioned to attack enemy shipping and aircraft. These guns were often hauled by Sd.Kfz.6 and Sd.Kfz.11 artillery tractors.

(**Above**) A Schwimmwagen Type 166 amphibious car of a Panzer division staff passes through a checkpoint. The vehicle is painted in overall dark sand colour. Behind the car are motorcycles and other various vehicles.

(**Above**) An 8.8cm FlaK gun can be seen halted in the desert being unlimbered from an Sd.Kfz.11 artillery tractor. The mighty 8.8cm FlaK gun was used in several roles during the war. It was arguably the most effective anti-aircraft and anti-tank gun used in the desert. Where the terrain was often flat and open, it allowed the long-range performance of the gun to be decisive. These guns were positioned all over the front lines for air-defence and were lethal to enemy aircraft. As the enemy air force increased in size and inflicted ever greater casualties on German positions, so the need for more 8.8cm FlaK guns increased.

(**Opposite, above**) A crewmember of a well-stocked Pz.Kpfw.III sits on the turret front surveying the terrain ahead.

(**Opposite, below**) An Sd.Kfz.251 Ausf.B armoured personnel carrier advances along a road. It was primarily the success of the Sd.Kfz.251 in the early war years that afforded halftracks a frontline combat role alongside the Panzer in the desert.

(**Opposite, above**) A column of armoured vehicles, predominately Pz.Kpfw.IIIs, advance along a road. The second and fifth vehicle in the column is a *Leichter Panzerspähwagen* (Fu) Sd.Kfz.223 (armoured radio car). It had a frame antenna and a 30-watt FuG 10 medium-range radio set. Later versions were equipped with a better 80-watt FuG 12 radio set. It was armed with an MG 34 machine gun and was manned by a crew of three including the radio operator.

(**Above**) Crewmembers standing next to their Pz.Kpfw.III out in the open desert. Note the water bottles festooned to the turret side. Water was a major commodity for the *Afrika Korps*, more important than fuel. Tank crews would carry huge quantities of water onboard.

(**Opposite, below**) The crew of an Sd.Kfz.251/1 Ausf.C armoured personnel carrier can be seen inside their vehicle. Note the mounted MG 34 machine gun with splinter shield.

The withdrawal of Rommel's forces: a column of Pz.Kpfw.IIIs pass under the triumphal arch built by the Italians on the Via Balba.

(**Opposite, above**) An Sd.Kfz.7 on the move pulling an 8.8cm FlaK gun to the front during operations in Libya in 1942. Whilst this prime mover was used to move troops from one part of the front to another and tow both artillery and FlaK guns, it also became the basis of a number of FlaK variants based on 2cm and 3.7cm FlaK types. The Sd.Kfz.7/1 was armed with a 2cm Flakvierling 38 quadruple and the Sd.Kfz.7/2 variant was armed with a single 3.7cm FlaK 36 gun.

(**Opposite, below**) A well-stocked Pz.Kpfw.III has halted. Behind the tank is a Funkpanzerwagen Sd.Kfz.251 radio command vehicle. This command halftrack with frame antenna included additional radio equipment as well as a combination of the earlier Fu-1, Fu-5, Fu-7, Fu-11 or Fu-12 radio transmitters, plus decoding equipment. It was often unarmed and carried command pennants and markings as it was used by senior commanders. Quite regularly these vehicles would be seen with reconnaissance vehicles and motorcycle dispatch riders that would collate information and directly send it back to the command halftrack.

The withdrawal of Rommel's forces: an Opel Blitz truck and motorcycle rider passing under the triumphal arch built by the Italians on the Via Balba.

Chapter Three

Destruction in Tunisia 1943

With the Anglo-Americans now threatening the very existence of the *Afrika Korps*, German High Command reacted quickly and upgraded its force, adding the XC Army Corps under General Walther Nehring. In addition to this, 5th Panzer Army was created and led by Colonel General Hans-Jurgen von Arnim. The new Panzer army was primarily built as a command formation to defend Tunisia. It was to fight alongside the Italian First Army as part of Army Group Africa.

To reinforce the Axis forces, tons of supplies were shipped across the Mediterranean to North Africa. Among the additional troops, artillery, FlaK and other weaponry were sixteen Pz.Kpfw.IIIs and three Tiger Is of the 501st Heavy Panzer Battalion or *Schwere Panzerabteilung* 501 (s-PzAbt501). These were the first elements of the battalion, along with four Pz.Kpfw.IIIs that were organised with other units into *Kampfgruppe* Lueder.

By early January 1943 the strength of s-PzAbt 501 was eleven operational Tigers and sixteen Pz.Kpfw.IIIs. Two weeks later eight Tigers and eight Pz.Kpfw.IIIs were assigned to the 756th *Gebirgsjäger* Infantry Regiment and *Kampfgruppe* Lueder was re-established with five Tigers and ten Pz.Kpfw.IIIs, and an additional battalion comprising the 1st Battalion of the 69th Mechanised Infantry Regiment.

The Tiger would be used extensively in both offensive and defensive deployments in Tunisia. They were few in number, but were the most powerful tank in North Africa and would become revered among the Allies. With Axis forces now fighting a withdrawal from Libya into Tunisia, Rommel would owe much to the Tiger tank for its support on the battlefield.

The Tigers too were to play a crucial role in the *Afrika Korps*' main objective of reaching the port of Tunis. Tripoli had been the German's main supply line in North Africa, but on 23 January 1943, the Eighth Army captured the port. Rommel then decided that Tunis would become his supply line and intended to block the southern approach to Tunisia from Tripoli at Gabes. Allied troops, however, were determined to split the Axis forces in southern Tunisia from the forces further north, and cut the supply line to Tunis and starve the *Afrika Korps* of further supplies. On 30 January the

5th Panzer Army arrived at the eastern foot of the Atlas Mountains where Allied forces were dug in. The 21st Panzer Division then moved forward towards the town of Faid and engaged French troops, forcing them to withdraw. A week later six Tigers and nine Pz.Kpfw.IIs from the 1st Company of the 501st were attached to the 10th Panzer Division for Operation *Frühlingswind*. Near the town of Bou Thadi they joined *Kampfgruppe* Reimann. On 14 February they managed to smash through the Faid Pass and became embroiled in heavy fighting at Sidi Bou Zid. It was here that the Tigers managed to knock out twenty M4 Sherman tanks of the US 1st Armoured Division. On 26 February, the 501st was redesignated III/Panzer-Regiment 7 of 10 Panzer Division. For additional reinforcements each company received fifteen Pz.Kpfw.IVs.

Between January and April 1943 the Axis had sustained thousands of casualties, and armoured vehicle losses were great and replacements too small. Lack of fuel, not enough spare parts, and the lack of trained crews all played their parts in reducing the effectiveness of the Panzer units in Tunisia.

On 9 March Rommel left Tunisia to be replaced by General Jurgen von Arnim. What followed was a complete collapse of the *Afrika Korps* as it spread itself out 100 miles across northern Tunisia attempting to push towards the coast. The Allies continued pushing forward while German forces were either forced to retreat or be destroyed. The once-proud Panzer divisions of the *Afrika Korps* were now reduced to skeletal formations on a stricken field. They were not only outnumbered but seriously lacked fuel supplies, lubricants and ammunition. By May, most of the remaining armoured units continued to fight until they destroyed their equipment and surrendered.

On 6 May, the British captured Tunis, and American forces reached Bizerte. By 13 May 1943, the Axis forces in Tunisia finally surrendered, sealing the fate of the *Afrika Korps* for ever.

Schwerer Panzerspähwagen Sd.Kfz.234 8-Rad armed with the powerful short-barrelled 7.5cm KwK 37 L/24 cannon. This vehicle was based on the open-topped superstructure of the Sd.Kfz.263 (8-Rad) radio vehicle. This variant of the Sd.Kfz series entered service during 1942, and although it remained in use throughout the war, it was not used extensively in operations in North Africa. They were issued as a platoon of six vehicles in support of reconnaissance battalions.

(**Opposite, above**) An *Afrika Korps* crew tuck into their rations standing next to their Sd.Kfz.231 during a pause in the action in late 1942 early 1943. This eight-wheeled vehicle had six forward and six reverse gears and could be driven at the same speed both directions.

(**Opposite, below**) A variety of vehicles from the new 5th Panzer Army spread out across the desert. The tank nearest in the photograph is a stationary Pz.Kpfw.III. The new Panzer army was primarily built as a command formation for armoured units forming to defend Tunisia against Allied attacks. It was to fight alongside the Italian First Army as part of Army Group Afrika.

(**Above**) A number of different vehicles can be seen in the desert during a German and Italian withdrawal. The Axis forces made a fighting withdrawal to El Agheila with Rommel conducting a text-book retreat, destroying all equipment left behind and setting the land behind him with masses of mines and booby traps.

(**Above**) Photographed from a reconnaissance vehicle, probably a Storch aircraft, armoured vehicles in a column crossing the desert.

(**Opposite, above**) One of the new Tiger tanks sent to reinforce Axis forces in North Africa. Among the additional troops, artillery, FlaK and other weaponry there were sixteen Pz.Kpfw.IIIs and three Tiger Is of the 501st Heavy Panzer Battalion or *Schwere Panzerabteilung* 501. These were the first elements of the battalion, along with four Pz.Kpfw.IIIs, that were organised with other units into *Kampfgruppe* Lueder.

(**Opposite, below**) A Pz.Kpfw.III Ausf.N negotiates a gradient during early operations in Tunisia in 1943. The N variant was the final production version of the standard Panzer III and was armed with the short 7.5cm gun used on early versions of the Panzer IV. It served as a close support tank in the early Tiger companies. Note the installation of candle dischargers on the turret sides.

(**Opposite, above**) A Tiger tank has halted on a road and the local Tunisian inhabitants can be seen next to the vehicle. By early January 1943 the strength of *Schwere Panzerabteilung* 501 (sPzAbt.501) was eleven operational Tigers. The Tiger was used in a number of prominent roles in North Africa to counter heavier Allied armour.

(**Opposite, below**) A Tiger from sPzAbt.501 during operations in Tunisia in January 1943. These were undoubtedly formidable fighting machines whose arrival at the front was a welcome relief to the now hard-pressed *Afrika Korps*. However, with too few of them delivered, Tiger crews found that they were too thinly stretched to make any significant dent in the growing armoured strength of the Allies.

(**Above**) The crew of a Tiger I has halted near some vegetation during operations in Tunisia. This Tiger belongs to sPzAbt.501. When it was shipped to North Africa at the end of December 1942 it was initially numbered 132. It was then renumbered 732 after the Beja Mission.

(**Opposite, above**) Tiger tank 142 of the 1 *Kompanie* sPzAbt.501 on the advance in Tunisia. This tank was unloaded in Tunis and began operations in January. The first three Tigers of the 1 *Kompanie* were unloaded on 23 November in Bizerte in 1942 by the ship *Aspromonte*. The remaining Tigers were shipped separately with the next one arriving on 27 November in Tunis. The remaining Tigers were shipped to Bizerte, one on the 1st of December, one on the 6th, one on the 13th, four on the 25th, and five on the 8th of January 1943, one the 16th, and the last two on the 24th.

(**Above**) Out in the desert and an Sd.Kfz.263 (8-rad) radio vehicle can be seen. This frame antenna was similar but not identical to that seen on the Sd.Kfz.232 (8-rad). Its main differences were in the way it was mounted and the curved section aft on the starboard side. Each armoured reconnaissance squadron comprised one radio command vehicle, four armoured cars fitted with radio, one heavy troop of half a dozen six- or eight-wheeled cars, and two light troops, each of which had six four-wheeled cars.

(**Opposite, below**) A column of Pz.Kpfw.IVs obviously near a harbour on the advance. The nearest tank is an Ausf.G variant and identified by a single hatch lid and the triple smoke candle dischargers on the turret sides. The Panzer behind the leading vehicle is also an Ausf.G as it has Bosch headlamps on both fenders.

Four photographs showing an engine change being carried out on an early production Tiger I of sPzAbt 501 in Tunisia. The first photograph shows a truck rotating crane installing a Tiger I Maybach HL210 P45 engine. In the second image the maintenance personnel are seen huddled around the other engine, while another engineer can be seen working on a removed section of the engine deck. In the last two photographs the installation of the engine is complete and the Tiger crew are seen eating their rations. Of interest, note the captured American Dodge truck parked behind the Tiger.

(**Above**) *Panzerwaffe* officers confer standing next to what appears to be a Pz.Kpfw.III during operations in Tunisia in 1943. The men are wearing a variety of clothing including a grey-green M1940 greatcoat, British captured gear, and an M1940 motorcycle rubberised greatcoat.

(**Opposite, above**) Motorcyclists are seen supporting an armoured advance across some stony uneven ground during operations in Tunisia. Note the amount of personal supplies mounted on the rear of the motorcycle. The Panzer is a Pz.Kpfw.III, and leading the drive is an Sd.Kf.251 armoured personnel carrier.

(**Opposite, below**) An image showing one of the first Tiger Is to arrive in Tunisia in early 1943. This vehicle is part of the 1 *Kompanie* sPzAbt.501. Quite common on the Tigers during the early period was the large national cross insignia that can be seen painted on the side plate superstructure. Note the Feifel air pack filters that can just be seen on the rear edge of the superstructure.

(**Opposite, above**) The crew of a Tiger I during operations in early 1941 can be seen resting in the desert watching a Tunisian man with his camel passing by. The tank belongs to the sPzAbt.501 and has the tactical number 111 painted in red with a white outline on the turret side.

(**Above**) A column of Tiger I tanks passes other stationary armour. The Tiger I gave the *Afrika Korps* its first armoured fighting vehicle that mounted the powerful 8.8cm KwK 36 cannon. It was generally a mechanically reliable vehicle but was occasionally prone to track failures and breakdowns. It was also very expensive to maintain, and limited in range by its high fuel consumption. But on the whole it was a brilliant addition to Rommel's fighting force.

(**Opposite, below**) Out in the desert in 1943 is a *Schwerer Panzerspähwagen* Sd.Kfz.234/3. This machine served as a support vehicle for the reconnaissance vehicles. It mounted a short 7.5cm K51 L/24 gun installed in a raised open superstructure.

(**Opposite, above**) A photograph showing the initial deployment of one of the Tiger tanks in Tunisia in early 1943. The image shows the tank on its port side. It is probable that since the crew have dismounted the MG 34 onto a bipod next to the vehicle, its more than likely that the Tiger has become disabled. Note all the crew's belongings attached to the turret side, and the local vegetation applied to the Tiger for camouflage protection.

(**Opposite, below**) A Tiger passes a stationary motorcyclist as the tank negotiates a narrow Tunisian road during operations in early 1943. The sPzAbt.501 fought a number of hard battles between December 1942 and March 1943. By the end of February 1943 the sPzAbt.501 was attached to 7th Panzer Regiment with the aim of attacking deep into enemy positions.

(**Above**) Rommel seen pulling up in his staff car conferring with some of his men who have commandeered a US M3 halftrack. Behind the American vehicle are two Sd.Kfz.251 armoured personnel carriers following the column.

A Pz.Kpfw.III has halted in the desert and the commander surveys the terrain through a pair of 6 × 30 binoculars. Note the additional track links bolted to the turret sides, turret roof and front side armoured plates.

A Tiger I pulls alongside a staff car on a Tunisian road in January 1943. Note the canvas sheeting protecting the 8.8cm cannon's muzzle break from dust and sand. This early production model is also fitted with triple smoke candle dischargers which were mounted on the turret sides as a factory standard during this period.

Out in the desert is an S.Pz.Ap.Wg. (Fu) 232 (8-rad), operating as part of a reconnaissance battalion. It is equipped with a frame antenna. These heavy armoured reconnaissance vehicles were versatile on the battlefield and their rapid movement constantly kept the enemy off-guard, denying him any opportunity to regroup his forces into a defensive position. Note the amount of personal gear attached to the outside.

A 10.5cm le.FH18 gun crew in the desert during the initial stages of operations in Tunisia. The 10.5cm howitzer normally had a nine-man crew. The wheels on the artillery piece were heavy duty cast steel with a solid rubber rim. This design allowed the gun to be hauled at relatively high speed by motorized vehicles such as the halftrack, notably the Sd.Kfz.6 or Sd.Kfz.11 artillery tractor.

Three photographs showing the *Sturmpanzer* II Bison 15 cm sIG 33 auf *Fahrgestell Panzerkampfwagen* II (Sf). This vehicle was armed with a 15cm sIG 33 howitzer on the chassis of a Pz.Kpfw.II. Twelve of these converted tank killers were built at the end of 1941 and were shipped to North Africa in early 1942 where they formed *Schwere Infanteriegeschütz-Kompanie* (mot. S.) (Heavy Self-propelled Infantry Gun Company) 707 and 708. They were employed as close support mobile units. The former was assigned to Schützen-Regiment 155 and the latter to Schützen-Regiment 200, both belonging to the 90th Light Afrika Division. Both of these companies saw extensive action in Tunisia until May 1943.

(**Above**) A brief respite for a signals battalion. The soldiers are wearing the familiar tropical field cap associated with the *Afrika Korps*, which appears to be so bleached by the sun and heat that it looks noticeably white against their dark olive tunics.

(**Opposite, above**) A captured *Sturmpanzer* II Bison 15cm sIG 33 auf *Fahrgestell Panzerkampfwagen* II (Sf) next to the triumphal arch on the Via Balba. Canvas sheeting covers the open-topped compartment of the Bison. The fighting compartment and sides of the vehicle were lower than the front which made the crew vulnerable to small arms fire and shell fragments. Large hatches were added to the rear deck to improve the engine's cooling system. It is evident from the photograph that there has been significant fighting in the area.

(**Opposite, below**) A Tiger tank can be seen negotiating the local terrain during intensive operations in Tunisia in 1943. Over the coming weeks, numbers of Tiger tanks were reduced by the overwhelming strength of the Allied forces. By mid-March there were only eleven Tigers of the sPzAbt.501 remaining and these were attached to the sPzAbt.504, which was the second Tiger unit to be sent to Tunisia. This unit, which arrived in Tunisia on 12 March 1943, comprised twenty-five Pz.Kpfw.IIIs and eighteen Tigers, along with the battalion staff, workshop company, and 1 *Panzer-Kompanie*. The 2 *Panzer-Kompanie* remained in Sicily. The tank company had four platoons, each with two Tiger I tanks and two Pz.Kpfw.III support tanks. By 12 May 1943 all of the sPzAbt.504 Tigers were destroyed or captured.

(**Above**) A knocked-out Pz.Kpfw.III can be seen with debris from the tank littered around where shells have impacted the side of the vehicle ripping off its track and damaging other parts of the tank. The shockwave and the fragments of a shell piercing armour would kill or at least incapacitate the crew. If crewmembers managed to bail out, there was then the worrying prospect of running into enemy fire, as this panzer crewman found out. His corpse can be seen sprawled out, baking in the sun next to his disabled machine.

(**Opposite**) Inhabitants of a Tunisian town are intrigued by an abandoned Marder III. The Marder III tank destroyer added significant firepower to the German army, but offered little in the way of protection for the crew. The upper structure mounted the gun and an extended gun shield only gave limited protection. Armour protection ranged from 10mm to 50mm with no armour at all above and behind the gun compartment. The Marder was not intended as an assault vehicle nor was it a tank. Its purpose was to operate in urban areas or other close-quarter combat situations where it could bring fire against enemy armoured vehicles. But due to growing shortages of tanks, the Marder III was compelled to be integrated alongside existing Panzer regiments and fight as a tank. This caused such severe losses to the *Panzerjäger* that they never recovered.

A soldier can be seen standing next to a halted Pz.Kpfw.III during operations in Tunisia in late 1942 or early 1943.

An abandoned Pz.Kpfw.III in late 1942. The panzer is armed with the 5cm KwK 38 L/42 cannon. The gun was successful throughout operations in North Africa scoring sizable successes against the Allies. The tank was known by the British as the 'Mark III Special'.

An abandoned Pz.Kpfw.II. In North Africa. These tanks were very reliable but by 1942 became increasingly obsolete in the face of improved Allied tanks. As a result they were relegated mainly to the role of scout vehicles in armoured reconnaissance units.

A knocked-out Pz.Kpfw.IV in the desert in early 1943. During the last weeks of the campaign in North Africa, the remaining German armour continued to fight as a unit until they destroyed their equipment and surrendered. Although the campaign ended in May 1943, the *Panzerwaffe* still existed, but not as the offensive force they were when they first arrived on the shores of Tripoli in February and March 1941. The Panzer men of Rommel's *Afrika Korps*, in their brief and extraordinary existence, had won a reputation for daring and professionalism in combat. They had provided the backbone of Germany's offensive and then defensive action in Africa, and the crews fought with courage and zeal to the end.

Appendix I

Afrika Korps Order of Battle

15th Panzer Division (26 March 1941)

HQ
Mapping Detachment (mot.)
Motorcycle Platoon
8 Panzer Regiment
2 × Battalion
15 Schützen Brigade (mot.)
2 × Regiment
15 Motorcycle Battalion
3 × Motorcycle Company
Motorcycle Machine Gun Company
Support Company
33 Reconnaissance Battalion
Armoured Car Company
Motorcycle Company
Heavy Weapons Company
33 Artillery Regiment

Regimental Staff
3 × Battalion
Observation Company (mot.)
33 Panzerjäger Battalion
Panzerjäger Platoon
3 × Panzerjäger Company (mot.)
33 Pioneer Battalion
Pioneer Company (halftrack)
Pioneer Company (mot.)
Light Pioneer Supply Column (mot.)
33 Signals Battalion
Signals Company (mot.)
Radio Company (mot.)
Light Signals Supply Column (mot.)
Support & Supply Column

15th Panzer Division (23 October 1942)

HQ
Mapping Detachment (mot.)
8 Panzer Regiment
Regimental Staff
Panzer Maintenance Company
2 × Battalion
115 Panzergrenadier Regiment
Regimental Staff
Support Company (mot.)
3 × Battalion (mot.)
FlaK Company
Infantry Gun Company (mot.)

33 Artillery Regiment
Regimental Staff
3 × Battalion (mot.)
Battalion (self-propelled)
I/33 FlaK Regiment (mot.)
4 × Battery (mot.)
33 Pioneer Battalion (mot.)
3 × Pioneer Company (halftrack)
Light Pioneer Supply Column (mot.)
33 Panzerjäger Battalion
Signals Platoon (mot.)
Panzerjäger Company (mot.)

Panzerjäger Company (self-propelled)
33 Reconnaissance Battalion
Armoured Car Company
Infantry Company (halftrack)
Support Company (mot.)
Light Armoured Car Supply Column
Light Howitzer Battery (mot.)
Light Reconnaissance Supply Column

33 Signals Battalion
Telephone Company (mot.)
Radio Company (mot.)
Light Signals Supply Column (mot.)
33 Feldersatz Battalion
4 × Company
Supply & Support Units

21st Panzer Division (November 1941)

HQ
200 Mapping Detachment (mot.)
200 Communication Section (mot.)
200 Construction Section
5 Panzer Regiment
HQ
HQ Company
Light Armoured Platoon
Regimental Band
Maintenance Company
2 × Battalion
HQ Company
Light Armoured Platoon
Medium Armoured Company
3 × Light Armoured Company
104 Schützen Regiment
HQ Company (mot.)
Signals Platoon (mot.)
Motorcycle Platoon
Panzerjäger Platoon
2 Machine Gun Battalion
HQ Company (mot.)
2 × Motorcycle Platoon
3 × Company Support Company
Panzerjäger Platoon
Mortar Platoon
Support Company
Pioneer Platoon
2 × Panzerjäger Platoon
Mortar Platoon

8. Machine Gun Battalion
HQ Company (mot.)
2 × Motorcycle Platoon
Signals Platoon
3 × Company
Support Company
Panzerjäger Platoon
Mortar Platoon
Support Company
Pioneer Platoon
2 × Panzerjäger Platoon
Mortar Platoon
Panzerjäger Company
155 Artillery Regiment
3 × Battalion
HQ Company (mot.)
3 × Battery (mot.)
3 Reconnaissance Battalion
Signals Platoon
Light Supply Column (mot.)
Armoured Car Company
Motorcycle Company
Support Company
Pioneer Platoon
Panzerjäger Platoon
Infantry Support Platoon
200 Feldersatz Battalion
4 × Company
200 Pioneer Battalion
3 × Company

200 Signals Battalion
Radio Company
Signals Company
Light Supply Column (mot.)

39 Panzerjäger Battalion
Signals Platoon (mot.)
3 × Company (mot.)
Supply Troops

90th Light Division (August 1941 to September 1942)

1st and 2nd Battalion, 155th Motorised Infantry Regiment
1st and 2nd Battalion, 200th Motorised Infantry Regiment
1st and 2nd Battalion, 361st Motorised Infantry Regiment
1st Battalion, 190th Motorised Artillery Regiment, 8 × 10.5cm, 4 × 10K17
2nd Battalion, 190th Motorised Artillery Regiment, 12 × 7.62mm(r)
190th Panzerjäger Battalion, 18 × 5cm
190th Mot. FlaK Battalion, 12 × 20mm
1st Kompanie, 613rd Motorised Lt FlaK Battalion, 4 × 20cm
90th Feldersatz Battalion, 6Co
900th Pioneer Battalion
707th Heavy Art Co, 6 × SiG33
708th Heavy Art Co, 6 × SiG33
Elements of 580th Reconnaissance Battalion, 5Co
361st and 580th Artillery Batteries

Appendix II

Panzers Operational in Africa 1941–43

Panzerkampfwagen I (Sd.Kfz.101) Ausf.A and B
Panzerkampfwagen II (Sd.Kfz.121) Ausf.A, B and C
Panzerbefehlswagen (Sd.Kfz.265 Light Armoured Command Vehicle)
Panzerjäger I Ausf.B 4.7cm PaK(t)
Panzerbefehlswagen III Ausf.E & H (Sd.Kfz.266, 267 and 268)
Panzerkampfwagen III (Sd.Kfz.141) Ausf.F, G, H and J
Panzerkampfwagen III (Sd.Kfz.141/1) Ausf.L, M, and N
Panzerkampfwagen IV (Sd.Kfz.161) Ausf.D, E and F1
Panzerkampfwagen IV (Sd.Kfz.161/1) Ausf.F2 and G
Panzerkampfwagen IV (Sd.kfz.161/2) Ausf.H
Panzerkampfwagen VI 'Tiger I' (Sd.Kfz.181) Ausf.E

Panzerkampfwagen I (Pz.Kpfw.I)

Ausf.A
The Panzer I Ausf.A featured a crew of two, a driver and a commander, the latter also used as the gunner. The driver sat forward of the hull of the vehicle on the left, while the commander occupied the turret to the right. The tank was armed with two 7.92mm machine guns, each capable of firing 650 rounds per minute (simultaneously or individually), and could only be traversed manually by the commander.

Ausf.B
This variant had an air-cooled engine developing 100 horsepower. The gearbox was changed to a more reliable model. The larger engine required the extension of the vehicle's chassis by 40cm, and this allowed the improvement of the tank's suspension, adding another bogie wheel and raising the tensioner. The tank's overall weight was increased by 400kg.

Ausf.C
The Ausf.C was completely modified. It had a new chassis and turret, a new torsion-bar suspension and five interleaved road wheels. The armour thickness was increased

to 30mm, which was twice that of either the Ausf.A or B models. It was armed with EW 141 semi-auto cannon with a 50-round drum firing 7.92mm anti-tank shells.

4.7cm PaK (t) (Sf) auf Pz.Kpfw.I Ausf.B

Known as the *Panzerjäger* I, or tank hunter, this was the first in a series of Panzer destroyers. For its construction the turret was removed and a Czech 4.7cm PaK (t) anti-tank gun was installed. The gun was capable of 35 degrees of traverse and elevation from −8 degrees to +12 degrees. A total of 86 rounds were carried for the main gun.

15cm sIG 33 (Sf) auf Pz.Kpfw.I Ausf.B

This was known as the Bison. Mounting a 15cm heavy infantry gun, the sIG33 was installed inside a tall superstructure. Thirty-eight of these vehicles were converted from Ausf.B variants in February 1940. They served with six heavy SP infantry gun companies and remained in service until 1943.

Panzerkampfwagen II (Pz.Kpfw.II)

Ausf.A

The design of this tank was based on the Pz.Kpfw.I but was larger and with a turret mounting a 2cm KwK30 L/55 cannon. For local defence it was armed with the 7.92mm MG 34 mounted coaxially with the main gun. The vehicle's armour thickness comprised 14mm of slightly sloped homogeneous steel armour on the sides, front, and back, with 10mm of armour on the top and bottom. All production variants of the Pz.Kpfw.II were fitted with the 140 PS, gasoline-fuelled six-cylinder Maybach HL 62 TRM engine and ZF transmissions.

Ausf.B

The Ausf.B entered production in December 1937. It could be distinguished from the early Ausf.A variant by the addition of a low cupola on the turret, designed to improve the commander's view.

Ausf.C

This variant entered production in June 1938 and was very similar to the Ausf.B but with minor internal improvements. When production ended in the spring of 1940 it had been expected that the Ausf.F would soon follow it onto the production lines, but this was delayed until March 1941.

Panzerkampfwagen III (Pz.Kpfw.III)

Ausf.F

The Ausf.F was the first version of the Panzer III to be produced in large numbers. It was virtually identical to the Ausf.E, but with a different engine ignition system and air intakes. Just over 300 were produced with the 3.7cm KwK gun, while approximately 100 were built with the 5cm KwK L/42 and an external mantlet. Many of the tanks originally built with the 3.7cm gun were later modified to carry the 5cm gun.

Ausf.G

This variant was initially very similar to the Ausf.F. The first fifty were built with the 3.7cm gun, while the remaining 550 used the 5cm gun. The rear armour of the Ausf.G was increased to 30mm, and a pivoting visor was added for the driver.

Ausf.H

The H was similar to late production Ausf.Gs, with the same wider tracks and 5cm gun. Extra 30mm armour plates were attached to the front and rear of the hull and the front of the superstructure. Less than half of the original order were produced before it was replaced by the Ausf.J.

Ausf.J (5cm KwK L/42)

The first version of the Ausf.J saw the frontal armour on the hull and superstructure and the rear hull armour increased in thickness from 30mm to 50mm. Hitler had ordered the use of the longer 50cm KwK39 L/60, but 1,500 tanks had been produced using the short gun before that order was implemented.

Ausf.J (5cm KwK39 L/60)

The adoption of the longer L/60 gun at the end of 1941 helped restore the usefulness of the Panzer III against British and American tanks in North Africa.

Ausf.L

The Ausf.L was armed with the 5cm KwK39 L/60. It was given 20mm spaced armour on the superstructure front and mantlet and thicker frontal turret armour.

Ausf.M

The Ausf.M was very similar to the Ausf.L but with the addition of a wading kit which allowed it to pass through 4 or 5 feet of water without any special preparation.

Ausf.N

The Ausf.N was the final production version of the standard Panzer III and was armed with the short 7.5cm gun used on early versions of the Panzer IV. It served as a close support tank in the early Tiger companies.

Panzerkampfwagen IV (Pz.Kpfw.IV)

Ausf.D

The Ausf.D was a newly improved version of the Ausf.C. Designers reintroduced the hull machine gun and changed the turret's internal gun mantlet to an external one. The vehicle's armour was upgraded and its side plates were increased to 20mm. Some 248 of these variants were manufactured.

Ausf.F2

Up-gunned Pz.Kpfw.IV 7.5cm KwK 40 L/43. Three months after beginning production in May 1942, the Pz.Kpfw.IV Ausf.F2 was renamed Ausf.G. There was hardly any difference between the F2 and early Ausf.G models.

Ausf.G

Armour was up-graded to 80mm thick, vision ports on either side of the turret were created and on the right the turret front was removed, a rack for two spare road wheels was installed on the track guard on the left side of the hull, brackets for seven spare track links were added to the glacis plate, ventilation was improved for engine operating in high temperatures by creating slits over the engine deck to the rear of the chassis, cold weather performance was boosted by adding a device to heat the engine's coolant, and a starter fluid injector was installed. Later, side skirts or *schürzen* were installed on its sides and turret, in some the double hatch for the commander's cupola was replaced by a single round hatch, and the cupola was up-armoured. In April 1943, the KwK 40 L/43 was replaced by the longer 7.5cm KwK 40 L/48 gun, with a redesigned multi-baffle muzzle brake with improved recoil efficiency.

Ausf.H

The Ausf.H version entered production in April 1943 and received the designation Sd.Kfz.161/2. This variant saw the integrity of the glacis armour improved by manufacturing it as a single 80mm plate, and anti-magnetic mine paste or *zimmerit* was added to all the vertical services of the tank armour. The vehicle's side and turret was further protected by the addition of 5mm side skirts and 8mm turret skirts. Various other modifications included replacing the rubber return rollers with cast steel and the hull fitted with triangular supports for the easily-damaged side skirts.

Panzerkampfwagen VI (Pz.Kpfw.VI) Tiger I

Production of the Panzerkampfwagen VI Ausf.H Tiger began in August 1942. This 48-tonne vehicle was armed with a 56-calibre 8.8cm KwK 36 cannon. A combination of a flat trajectory from the high muzzle velocity and precision from Leitz *Turmzielfernrohr* TZF 9b sight (later replaced by the monocular TZF 9c) made it very accurate. The Tiger I had frontal hull armour 100mm (4 inch) thick, frontal turret armour of 100mm and a 120mm-thick gun mantlet. The vehicle had 60mm thick hull side plates and 80mm armour on the side superstructure, while turret sides and rear were 80mm. The top and bottom armour was 25mm thick. Its armoured plates were mostly flat, with interlocking construction. The Tiger was primarily moved to Tunisia in January 1943 in order to support the *Afrika Korps*.

Appendix III

Heavy and Light Armoured Vehicles Operational in North Africa 1941–43

Heavy Armoured Vehicles

Schwerer Panzerspähwagen (heavy armoured reconnaissance vehicle), covered the series of heavy four-wheel drive vehicles:

Schwerer Panzerspähwagen Sd.Kfz. 231 (8-rad)

Standard reconnaissance vehicle built from 1937 to 1941.

Schwerer Panzerspähwagen (Fu) Sd.Kfz. 232 (8-rad)

Comprised additional medium range radio sets and a large frame aerial. From 1942, a small star aerial replaced the frame aerial.

Schwerer Panzerspähwagen (7.5 cm) Sd Kfz. 233

Equipped with a short barrelled 7.5cm KwK 37 L/24 gun and based on the open-topped superstructure of the Sd.Kfz. 263 (8-Rad) radio vehicle. Supported reconnaissance battalions.

Schwerer Panzerspähwagen Sd.Kfz.263 reconnaissance (8-rad)

Open-topped fixed superstructure vehicle armed with a single 7.92mm MG 34 machine gun. A dedicated radio vehicle with aerial frame antennae.

Schwerer Panzerspähwagen Sd.Kfz.234

A completely new design and similar size and appearance to the Sd.Kfz.231. The most obvious external difference was the single-piece mudguards compared to the two-piece mudguards on the 232 series.

Schwerer Panzerspähwagen Sd.Kfz.234/1

Armed with a 2cm KwK38 L/55 and coaxial 7.92mm MG 34 or MG42 machine gun installed in a rotating six-sided open-topped turret. In order to protect the turret top against possible hand grenade attacks the armoured car had a wire mesh hood.

Schwerer Panzerspähwagen Sd.Kfz.234/2

Mounted the powerful 5cm KwK 39/1 L/60 canon, which was similar to that installed in the Pz.Kpfw.III medium Panzer. It was regarded as one of the most heavily armoured reconnaissance vehicles in the German arsenal during the first part of the war.

Schwerer Panzerspähwagen Sd.Kfz.234/3

Served as a support vehicle for the reconnaissance vehicles, was armed with a short 7.5cm K51 L/24 gun installed in a raised open superstructure.

Light Armoured Vehicles

Leichter Panzerspähwagen (light armoured reconnaissance vehicle) covered the series of light four-wheel drive vehicles:

Leichter Panzerspähwagen Sd.kfz.221 (4-Rad)

Manned by a two-man crew and armed with a single 7.92mm MG13 machine gun and later from 1938 an MG 34 machine gun mounted in the upper turret. Production of these vehicles ran from 1935 to 1940 and later in the war there were a number of them rearmed with the 2.8cm sPzB41 heavy anti-tank rifle in a modified turret.

Leichter Panzerspähwagen Sd.Kfz.222 (4-Rad)

Armed with a 2cm KwK30 L/55 cannon, initially with the MG13 and later replaced with the MG 34 and then modified with a KwK38.

Leichter Panzerspähwagen (Fu) Sd.Kfz.223

This armoured radio car was produced from 1936 to January 1944 and built with similar characteristics to the Sd.Kfz.221 but with the addition of a frame antenna and a 30-watt FuG 10 medium-range radio set. Later versions were equipped with a better 80-watt FuG 12 radio set. Originally armed with a 7.92mm MG13 machine gun, in 1938 an MG 34 machine gun was installed. The crew was increased to three by the addition of a radio operator.

Kleiner Panzerfunkwagen Sd.Kfz.260/261

Unarmed radio vehicle built in early 1941, in production until early 1943. It had long range radio equipment installed with and a large frame antenna bolted over the vehicle. Its intended use was for signals. The Sd.Kfz.260 was equipped with radio sets to communicate with aircraft, while the other version of this vehicle, the Sd.Kfz.261, was built primarily to communicate with the ground army by radio sets.

Halftracks Operational in North Africa 1941–43

Variants of the Sd.Kfz.251

251/1a Schützen Panzerwagen (Ausf.A, B, C, D)

The basic vehicle was designed to carry ten riflemen and all their equipment plus a two-man crew consisting of driver and commander. Two MG 34s were fitted, one sweeping the front and one on a more movable arm at the rear. The introduction of the Ausf.B saw the introduction of a protective MG shield. The MG 34 was later replaced by the MG 42 with all Ausf.D versions having MG 42s.

251/1b Schützen Panzer Wg (Ausf.A, B, C)

The same as version 251/1a, but this vehicle carried only nine riflemen. In addition a heavy mount for the MG 34 was fitted.

251/3 Funk Panzer Wg (Ausf.C, D)

Introduced in mid-1940 to act as a prime mover for the leIG 18 light infantry gun. The vehicle was fitted with a specially strengthened towing mount. It could also carry 120 rounds of ammunition. The towing mount was later adapted to accommodate various AT guns such as the 37mm PaK 36, 50mm PaK 38, 75mm PaK 40 and the heavier infantry gun the 105mm leFH 18. In early 1943 the 251/3 reverted to a communications role. The vehicle was refitted with a variety of radios and antenna.

251/6 Kommand Panzer Wg (Ausf.A, B, C, D)

Initially this vehicle was only used by divisional commanders, but as more vehicles became available they were used more extensively. The vehicle was equipped with various decoding and deciphering apparatus and a variety of radios and antenna. The vehicle carried a crew of up to eight and was armed with one forward firing MG 34.

251/7 Pioneer Panzer Wg (Ausf.C, D)

This vehicle was introduced to provide transport for engineer sections and their equipment. Two metal bridge-arcs could be carried on the sides. In addition assault boats and demolition stores were also carried.

251/8 Krankenpanzerwagen (Ausf.B, C, D)

This vehicle was introduced as an armoured ambulance. It could carry two stretchers and four seated wounded. Later models had redesigned doors to allow for easy entry and exit. Had a FuG5 when it was issued to HQ Company or Panzer detachment.

251/10 Schütz Panzer Wg 3.7cm Pak (Ausf.A, B, C, D)

This vehicle was introduced in 1940 as a platoon leader's vehicle. Initially the standard 37mm PaK 36 was simply fitted on top of the armour above the driver and co-driver. Later a mounting for the gun and an armoured shield were fitted. The vehicle carried up to six men and 168 rounds of 3.7cm ammunition.

251/11 Fernsprech Panzer Wg (Ausf.C)

This vehicle was introduced in mid-1942 to serve as an armoured cable-laying vehicle. In the crew compartment a cabinet with cable reels and equipment replaced the right-hand benches. Three cable-laying units were fitted in the vehicle and the crew used poles to hang the cable in trees. It carried a crew of five.

251/12 Messtr u Geraete Panzer Wg (Ausf.B, C)

This vehicle was introduced in early 1942 as an artillery survey section vehicle. Specialised artillery observation units were equipped with this vehicle to carry their equipment. The vehicle carried a crew of six.

251/13 Schallaufn Panzer Wg (Ausf.C)

This vehicle was equipped with specialised instruments to record and examine the sound of enemy artillery batteries and then locate their positions.

251/14 Schallausw Panzer Wg (Ausf.C)

This vehicle was equipped with specialised sound ranging instruments to interpret the sound of enemy artillery and then locate their positions.

251/15 Lichtausw Panzer Wg (Ausf.C)

This vehicle was equipped with flash spotting instruments to interpret the flashes of enemy artillery then locate their position.

251/17 Mittlerer Schützenpanzerwagen (20mm) Flak

This vehicle was introduced in mid-1942. It was fitted with either a 2cm FlaK 30 or FlaK 38. Vehicles mounting the FlaK 38 often had a bulging superstructure with drop-down sides to enable a better traverse of the gun. Although designed for anti-aircraft protection, the weapons could also be used in the ground role.

251/19 Mittlerer Fernsprech-Betriebspanzerwagen (Ausf.D)

This vehicle was introduced in mid-1942 to serve as an armoured telephone relay unit. It carried a crew of five and operated in unison with the 251/11.

Variants of the light Sd.Kfz.250

Sd.Kfz.250/1 Schützenpanzerwagen

Introduced in early 1940 the basic model was used to carry a half section for reconnaissance tasks. It was also used as a platoon and company commander's vehicle. The command vehicle was equipped with various decoding and deciphering apparatus and a variety of radios and antenna. It was equipped with either one or two MG 34s on pivot mounts. The vehicle could carry a crew of six.

Sd.Kfz.250/2 Fernsprechpanzerwagen

Introduced in early 1941 this vehicle was introduced as an armoured telephone cable layer and was also used as an observation vehicle. It could lay up to three cables at a time and carried a crew of four.

Sd.Kfz.250/3 Funkpanzerwagen

Communications vehicle introduced in early 1941, fitted with a variety of radios and antenna, carrying a crew of four.

Sd.Kfz.250/4 Truppenluftschützpanzerwagen

Introduced in early 1941 this vehicle was an air liaison and observation vehicle. It was used by *Luftwaffe* forward air controllers to assist aircraft and talk them onto their targets. Crew of four.

Sd.Kfz.250/5 Beobachtungspanzerwagen

Introduced in mid-1941 this vehicle was a forward observation vehicle for assault gun batteries. Crew of four.

Sd.Kfz.250/6 Munitionspanzerwagen

Introduced in early 1941 this vehicle served as an ammunition carrier for assault guns. It could be fitted internally to carry either 70 rounds for the short 7.5cm StuK 37 L/24 gun or 60 rounds for the long 7.5cm StuK 40 L/43.

Sd.Kfz.250/9 Schützenpanzerwagen 2cm

This vehicle was introduced in mid-1942 to replace the wheeled armoured cars which were unsuitable for the terrain in Russia. The turret assembly of the Sd.kfz.222 was fitted onto the top of the superstructure, which was roofed to accommodate it. Crew of three.

Sd.Kfz 250/10 Schützenpanzerwagen 3.7cm PaK

This vehicle, introduced in late 1940, had the standard 3.7cm PaK 36 simply fitted on top of the armour above the driver and co-driver. Later a mounting for the gun and an armoured shield were fitted. The vehicle carried a crew of three.

Sd.Kfz 250/12 Messtruppanzerwagen

This vehicle was introduced in early 1942 to replace the Sd.Kfz.251/13. It was used as an artillery survey and observation vehicle. Crew of four.

Notes